365 Days with Source

Daily Enlightenment & Inspiration

Elliott and Diane Jackson

365 Meditational Quotes

Based on information sent from Source in

From God to You: Absolute Truth

&

The Sapiential Discourses
Universal Wisdom
Book Series

By Elliott Eli Jackson

Photographs & Digital Images, Pixamay - https://pixabay.com/, 4/6/2018

Copyright © 2018 by Elliott Eli Jackson

All Rights Reserved.

No part of this book may be used or reproduced in any manner without prior written permission from the publisher, except in the case of brief quotations embodied in critical reviews and articles.

The scanning, uploading, and distribution of this text via the Internet or via any other means without the permission of the publisher is illegal and punishable by law. Please purchase only authorized electronic editions, and do not participate in or encourage electronic piracy of copyrighted materials. Your support of the author's rights is appreciated.

ISBN: 9781980805922

Imprint: Independently published

Many throughout the world have come to embrace the truths from Source in Elliott's books. The wonderful words from Source are revitalizing and life-changing. The Source of all things desires for you to know that there is nothing that you cannot do.

The purpose of this book is for motivation and meditation. The quotes are a daily tools to assist you in raising your personal vibrational level to create a happier, healthier life.

Elliott and Diane travel across America and the world presenting the life-changing words of Source in seminars. Attend one for yourself!

Visit www.quantummatrixcenter.com

Day 1

You must begin to embrace and understand that you are created in OUR image. You are Creator, which means there is nothing you can't do!

Day 2

Come softly unto yourself. Be gentle in speech and demeanor when necessary, yet speak your truth with force and love. When you remember this, it will assist you in all your relationships and in understanding your others. Fore, all others are you!

Day 3

You are the whole self and the center of self all at once and forever. The self is your Spirit and is autonomous from the rest of your physical being (body, mental, emotional). Yet it is fully integrated into such.

Day 4

Even when it seems dark there is always Light.
Even when you feel there is not hope there is
LOVE.

Day 5

Even when you think you can't go on,
there is GOD!
You are God and God is you!
Keep your faith in self, in light and love,
and you will see all will be well.

Day 6

There are walls of Love just waiting for you.

There are mountains of joy, success and peace. Won't you accept them?

Step out of your fear.

Remember!

Day 7

Each moment gives way to the next and the next is the same as the prior!

Day 8

Peace is the absence of despair, hopelessness, turmoil, unnecessary friction, and hate.

Are you at Peace?

Day 9

Today, know that when you do something, i.e. make a decision, take an action or whatever, insure that it is in the highest good for yourself and others.

Day 10

You are the embodiment of US adapted to your current environment. You are a fourfold being ever-changing!

Day 11

Unless one understands the basis and Complexity of self, one will never be able to Raise their vibrational level.

Day 12

To be able to fully grasp self and the divine is surely a blessing. This understanding allows one to better understand others, whom are in essence yourself.

Day 13

Remember,

You are spirit encased within flesh and blood!

Remember!

Day 14

Even when it seems dark, there is always Light. Even when you feel there is not hope, there is Love. Even when you think you can't go on - There is GOD!

Day 15

... you must be able to function within yourself rather than the continued attempts to control the outcomes of others.

Day 16

WE, which you call GOD, accept and LOVE all without Exception or Condition!

Day 17

WE come to You during this critical time in humankind's history/herstory to dispel the Lies and Misinformation given to you about whom WE are and who YOU Are! YOU are Creator!

Day 18

Why is it that many of you think that if you have three dollars in your pocket you are broke and if you have three hundred dollars you are OK?

Day 19

WE tell you: The idea that you must have a lot of money to be validated is a concept and notion that springs from the mental portion as seen through your holographic view of self.

Day 20

You are a

CREATOR

no less than US.

You are Light and Love!

Day 21

WE are saying just pray. Just talk to US no matter the case, no matter the cause. WE are always here for you—always! In your darkest hour, come; in joy and frustration come.

Day 22

When you surrender to self

the sky will open up to you.

The stars will shine brighter than ever before

and your life will no longer be your own.

You will serve your fellow man!

Day 23

YOU play an important role

in the Grand Scheme of it all!

Remember!

Day 24

WE tell you,

your children watch everything you do.

They learn from you, mimic you.

So ask yourself, What am I Teaching them?

Is it of Love and Light?

Day 25

The exceptional person

that you see in the mirror is

YOU!

Day 26

What you do Today determines your Tomorrow!

What you do Tomorrow is linked to your Yesterday!

Yesterday - Today - Tomorrow

Day 27

You know there is much to do for

Yourself and your Earth.

Be involved with self.

Be involved with your Earth!

Day 28

WE tell you, all seekers of truth should have some Hematite for grounding and protection. Where's yours?

Day 29

You are doing better than you think!

Never beat-up on yourself.

Day 30

WE tell you that in your current physical existence you were not made to be alone.

Remember!

Day 31

Be it known to you that prayer is an important,

Integral, part of your human existence.

Prayer is essential!

Have you talked to US today?

Day 32

WE tell you, the conscious

folds into the unconscious;

thus, you indeed wish

and bring things into reality.

Day 33

All you have to do is Call.

WE are Always Listening.

WE are Always on Call.

Day 34

Ensure that the freedom to express oneself verbally is respected. Honor this!

Day 35

Make noise about issues and the like

that you don't agree with.

Do this for All Injustices and it will catch on.

WE promise!

Day 36

Yes, Ask and it is Given.

However, some action must be taken!

Remember!

Day 37

What will happen if and when you obtain the truthful information about self? You are beautiful and wonderful. Your plans will begin to take their full scope and potential. Then weight loss or gain, or whatever you desire, will happen or occur.

Day 38

All of you can change yourself

and your Earth.

WE believe in You.

Day 39

The sad situations on your home, your planet, your Earth, are an effect of low vibrations. Therefore, as many raise their vibrational level, many sad situations will disappear.

Day 40

Treat yourself to something good today! It will help you feel better. And if you already feel good, you will just feel that much better.

Day 41

Give your loved ones a call Today.

You will bring joy to their spirit.

They may not tell you, yet WE tell you it will

uplift their very Soul.

Day 42

The human body was and is not physiologically designed to eat massive quantities of meat. Yet WE inform you that it is okay to do so, for you have created the eating of meat. It would be a good idea, however, to eat small portions.

Day 43

Earth you are.

Earth is in you and all around you.

You are a part of it and it is a Part of You!

Day 44

If you are not taking very good care of self, it may be time to do so! Remember, so as a man or woman Thinketh so they become!

Day 45

All on Earth make mis-takes.

Each day is a new opportunity to raise your personal vibrational level, change direction, and take higher vibrational actions that will not harm yourself or others.

Day 46

Remember, just as it is with the Wind, the Closer that all of you are together, The Stronger You Are!

Day 47

No other creator on your planet worries. The trees and flowers do not worry for water, the grass does not worry if the sun will shine, and the rocks do not worry if someone walks upon them. Therefore, know that there is nothing that you should worry about.

Day 48

You are a Healer. Yes, it is you that heals self. No one else can heal you. WE tell you, all the power is within you. It always has been. It is time for you to realize such.

Day 49

War is a disadvantage of being outside the Oneness.

War is a cerebrally distorted adaptation of what many of you consider to be your morality.

Day 50

Say to yourself each day -

Today is a beautiful day as are all days!

Day 51

Be of Good Cheer and Happy Heart,

Compassionate to Yourself

and Your Others!

Day 52

WE will love you in the face of come what may,

whoever you are, wherever you are,

however you are.

It is a law of OUR Universe.

Day 53

Money was created to be used, so use it.

The more of it you get,

the more you should give away. It will come

back to you, for it loves you just as you

love it. You are, after all, its Creator!

Day 54

Don't you understand the power

that you have?

Day 55

The Spiritual Revolution is happening Now on Your planet. It is and does bring about great change. It will change many of your ideologies, economies, political structures, and institutions. This Change will be Forever!

Day 56

Today - If it is possible

tell your mother and father

that you love them.

Day 57

Remember, it is the rain

that causes the flowers to grow.

It is you that brings smiles

to the faces of the ones that love you!

Day 58

In the beginning, there was not darkness, there was Light and Love. WE are Light, You are Light. WE are Love; You are Love.

Day 59

Remember,

Woman brings about life.

Woman is the glue that holds the bonds of family together!

Day 60

You and your kind can replace much needed missing or depleted vitamins and minerals through treatments using essential oils and other homeopathic medications.
Check it out!

Day 61

Each of you play a part in your Wonderful World!

Day 62

Children are the future.

Guide them in the proper direction and they will bring peace and stability to Earth.

Day 63

Eat the best foods for you. You know what they are. Eat that cake, if you desire. Yet, know this. The whole cake may not be best for you. Eat candy, why not? It would, however, not be best for you to eat the whole box in one sitting.

Day 64

Treat the friends you have as you treat yourself. Encourage them to be their best, reinforce to them that they are the creators of their own destiny. Spend time with them, support them in their endeavors.

Day 65

Love

The guiding force behind All great things!

Remember!

Day 66

Your dreams and goals are first imagined,

then the faith that they can be comes into play,

then comes the action.

Follow your Dreams!

Day 67

Do you know

Your thoughts produce your dreams?

Day 68

Sleep and dreaming are but two of the processes that your wonderful being experiences. Try to remember your dreams tonight.

Day 69

WE ask all of you to not succumb to fear. People will come up with all sorts of theories to spread fear. Nevertheless, you have nothing to fear.

Day 70

WE desire for you to love your neighbors as self because they are you. This is what WE have been trying to tell you throughout the ages.

Day 71

Before the beginning of human and animal life on Earth, there was an arrangement. It was a universal, spiritual, masterful arrangement between the spirit of the feminine and the spirit of the masculine, the yin and the yang, the god and the goddess.

Day 72

At one time, you too were capable, and still are, of thought transference (telepathy), so if you really work at it and remember who you really are, you will be able to use this gift from US to help yourself and others.

Day 73

Ensure, if you have children of school age that they complete their homework before they play or do any other activities. You can do it! Assist them with their homework; it is not too hard for you. All the while, remind them that they deserve the best that life has to offer.

Day 74

Spend time in silence with US.

Things will become clear

and the path to the answers

that you seek will appear.

Day 75

All great men and women acknowledge

US.

Do You?

Day 76

Time well spent brings about rewards

of the Spirit and Soul!

Sleeping, Working, Praying, Meditating,

Healing Self and Others, Loving, Sharing,

Caring, Cleansing, Laughing, Playing,

Reflecting, Eating, Creating!

Day 77

How do you process your feelings?

Day 78

Remember, your feelings are valid.

Feel them, process them,

and then Move On!

Day 79

The nearest descriptive word of a
Twin Flame in your current understanding is
Duplication, as you understand this term,
of your Soul or Spirit. Receive the gifts they
give you for what they are worth
and be Grateful.

Day 80

Have you noticed?

Collectively and rapidly,

as compared to man's history up until now,

the Mass Consciousness on Earth

is reaching towards new heights, and it is good.

Day 81

Faith can and will cause your humankind

to spring into more exercise and better

eating habits, becoming more aware

of the things you place within your sacred self.

Day 82

Did or have you exercised today?

Did or are you going to eat balanced meals today?

Day 83

The spirit is remembering that life, in all its full

glory and manifestations,

is to be lived and enjoyed.

Are you living your Life?

Day 84

Nothing can tame the Spirit,

and that Spirit is seeking Peace

and connection with others on

a Deeper Level.

Day 85

All of you are working to get back to

the original state of Oneness.

It is the major unseen Process

in the midst of all that you do.

Day 86

Please go to your mirror and say to self —

I AM Worthy!

I AM Wonderful!

I AM Magnificent!

Day 87

Today sit down and make -

A six month plan!

A one year plan!

A five year plan!

You will be surprised what will happen if you follow them.

Day 88

Even when you think you are not doing anything, Spirit is sending out Light and Love, and connecting with other Spirits.

Fore, that is what Spirit does.

Day 89

Your planet has been visited many times by your others from other planets, spaces and places. WE inform you that it is most arrogant for any of your species to, by any stretch of the imagination, think that there are no other intelligent, progressive life forms elsewhere in the universes.

Day 90

Remember -

There is only Fear and Love.

Which one are you operating out of Today?

Day 91

It is important to Remember that Freedom of Choice is always an option. Even those that you think are not capable of choosing, including Children. Fore, the Spirit of anyone can at any given moment Prevail and Excel.

Day 92

If you notice, you will see stars in your eyes!

Day 93

If you could see your spirit, you would see wonderful colors and dynamic lights. You would be able to see great expanses.

Day 94

The soul or spirit is able to discern all things. It is able to predict the outcomes of any given situation and navigate properly for positive end results. Now, the problem being, most of you allow the mental portion of your being to direct and/or dictate outcomes and decisions.

Day 95

Open-mindedness should be approached from the vantage point of looking at yourself from the outside. Imagine you are viewing your own actions/behaviors on a consistent basis. If you visualize this, you may not be prone to doing things that you really do not desire to do or doing things that you may regret later.

Day 96

You reach more people on the face of this Earth than you can ever imagine. Therefore, sometimes you do not have to do anything but be.

Day 97

You are capable of

great things within and outside

of your physical being.

Day 98

Think you not, that lower portions of US will not send to and towards you A Human Substance? Just when you are at the door of discovery, lower portions can cause the very person whom may keep you from turning the corner to show up. Be Alert!

Day 99

Yes, there are Mermaids. They are not a myth. They are real, just as real as you. Remember, there is more to the universes than meets the Eye.

Day 100

Seeking a Mate? It is purity of Spirit you should seek. Seek the spirit which takes you back through time and space, no matter the physique, the height, the hair, the nose, or the color of skin. This one will bring you love, hope, and compassion. They will bring the high and low of your being out for scrutiny and refining.

Day 101

Parenting is one of the most important, if not the most important, aspect of your being that you have created. It is truly a complex process within your societies and yet simple. Now, think about the term yet simple!

Day 102

Whatever faith you may take hold of,

Care for the weak and downtrodden, and

assist others in raising their personal vibration.

Day 103

If you can, take a walk today. Look at the faces of others as you pass them, see the face of God in all. Notice those hanging their heads, say Good Morning or Good Afternoon to them. WE promise, when you return home you will feel good knowing that you have touched others this day!

Day 104

Pain and suffering, part of your human condition. Why? You wouldn't appreciate other conditions - joy, good health, love, success, all emotions, unless you experience the opposites. You wouldn't be able to understand who you are until you know who you are not.

Day 105

Say and know today - Creator you Are!

Day 106

Yes, you need to Hydrate. However, consider, your body is at least 60% water. WE tell you, you have a much higher percentage. Therefore, should one of you consume eight glasses of water a day? WE think Not! If you are pregnant or lactating you could drink that. Otherwise - No!!

Day 107

Romantic relationships or any others should be based in trust. Is trust given or earned? It is both. You, automatically, give trust. You have no choice. It is there up-front at all times, until one is proven to have taken advantage of your trust, after which time, it must be earned back.

Day 108

Let your love flow because you wish to empower that one to become his or her highest self.

Day 109

WE love You. You deserve the Best. And You shall have it, if You but ask and take the steps necessary to obtain such.
WE will Help; WE will assist You in obtaining a Higher State of Being.

Day 110

Spiritual solutions take you to Acceptance. This universally grants the true healing processes to begin. It is through Acceptance that many of what you consider unbearable situations become bearable.

Day 111

There is no set way to pray,

you can just talk to US.

WE will listen anytime, anywhere, any matter.

A deep connection or bond

is formed during prayer.

Day 112

Always show compassion, justice, humility, kindness, and other positive actions and behaviors in all you do.

It is the Way Of A Master.

Day 113

Your dreams are fascinating and revealing, and many of you think that reality is far from your dreams. Yet WE tell you, in most cases, dreams are to become your reality, or have been in some respect within the realm of either your present, past, or future lives.

Day 114

Your Spirit always accepts the Truth when it is placed in front of it, yet the mental and emotional are different. They accept slowly because they are the portions of your being that have been most affected by the lies and mis-conceptions that have been given to you in the past.

Day 115

Channeling is looked upon with great disbelief, yet it is the most occurring or reoccurring para-normal activity that there is. WE tell you, all books, music, and art are Channeled. All of your ideas are Channeled.

Day 116

The Female is the Leader - Fore, in her true state she is compassionate, caring, passive, emotionally driven, patient, erogenous, kind, thoughtful, direct, communal, rational, understanding, and unvarnished. She is able to quickly cascade higher spiritual thoughts into the mental.
If the feminine leads it brings about peace.

Day 117

The masculine is the head - Fore, in his true state, he is intrepid, bold, loving, protective, alert, erect, invested, accountable, slaving (to a defect at times if unbridled), tense, humble, disparate, cautious, basic, obvious, policing. This is to say he is able to defend and protect the relationship's unity and integrity.

Day 118

Fear is a lower vibrational belief!

Day 119

- I Am Starseed

(precursor to Indigo, born 1950 thru 1975)

* I Am Indigo Blue

(majority born after 1975 - a few exceptions)

◊ I Am a new Star Implant

(began coming to Earth January 1st, 2016)

Destined to Change the World!

Day 120

Everything accomplished on Earth began with

I Am

Day 121

Mary Magdalene the Wife of Jesus

Investigate Please

Day 122

All the Great Ones on Your Planet

have been Keepers of I Am.

Are You?

Day 123

Think about the Deer for a moment. They may appear to be inattentive or laissez faire in regards to what is occurring around them. Yet they are always alert and on guard, ready to spring away. So should you be in regards to those around You! Be on guard against those that are vexatious to your spirit. Be ready to Remove yourself from their presence.

Day 124

Faith is action and movement propelled by belief. It is wonderful within itself and can overcome anything.

Day 125

Tears are cleansing. Tears release toxins and are capable of purging the Soul and Spirit!

Day 126

It may be time for some personal

introspection and thought.

You may need to

purge your physical body or discard

some old, outdated ways of thinking.

Day 127

Your dreams hold many keys and connections to your current relationships and all of your life issues. This is why it is important for you to understand some of the aspects of your dreams.

Day 128

There has been a concerted effort by many throughout time to confuse and mislead the masses with ideas and concepts that are only conjecture and particles of the truth.
That time is nearing its end.

Day 129

Are you able to Express your Feelings to others?

Are you one who has issues with Expression?

Day 130

Know that you are important.

Understand that your feelings count.

Know that you are equal to all.

Understand that your opinion matters.

Know that there is nothing to fear.

Day 131

You have been taught or trained that God, Source, WE do not speak directly to you now, but did or may have in the past.

Lies - WE are speaking to you right Now!

Day 132

The first stage of prayer, Adoration: letting US know you love US and yourself.

Day 133

The use of sunscreen has increased. More and more people are pouring into gyms and doing cardiovascular exercises, and many are cleansing their digestive systems.

How About You?

Day 134

What you think or do not think about US does matter. Moreover, what you think formalizes who you are and your relationship to the world around you, and with the external portions of the universe that you cannot see. So, keep it simple. WE are Love!

Day 135

Angels are not supernatural because they have superpower, for you do too. They are supernatural to you because their powers or gifts are different from yours.

Day 136

The moment right now is all you have.

And right now, in this moment, all is well.

Day 137

Quantum Touch and Quantum Healing are methods of assisting one in healing themselves. And, yes, they are carried out with the use of the human hand.

Maybe you should look into them!

Day 138

There are no Sins. However, there are Seven Lower Vibrational Decisions one can make.

1. Excessive Lust - You should look this up in *The Sapiential Discourses*, Book III, pg. 111.

Day 139

Did you know?

Certain oils, crystals, tones, sounds, and touch are able to direct waves correctly towards certain portions of the brain.

Day 140

The Stream of Consciousness is a reflection or mirror of all your positive or negative beliefs, ideas, and concepts combined.

And, according to what the majority of you are thinking and doing, at any given moment, it can cause things to be or not to be.

Day 141

When is the last time you treated yourself to something? WE don't mean your husband or your wife, your children or your friends.

WE mean YOU!

Day 142

Some will say you can't do anything about planet Earth, about the face of change. WE, All There Is, Was, and Ever Shall Be, are telling you they know not what they speak. You are Pure Creators and have the choice to Create as you Wish. Create a Peaceful World. You Can!

Day 143

Do You Have a Best Friend? All of you should - not your husband or wife, or a family member, a Best Friend.

Today, let your best friend know how much they mean to You!

Day 144

Ponder on how Birds soar effortlessly in the Sky. WE tell you, you should and need to be like them, Soaring in all aspects of your life. And of course, if you are not, Why Not?

Day 145

Love is all there is, so act accordingly. When you grasp this Our children, hate and mistreatment of your sacred self and others will fade away as the mist on the leaves dissipate when the Sun hits the dew. You will find true happiness and raise your vibrational level. This is Our hope and desire for all of YOU!

Day 146

Notice the intricacies in Your Finger. See the lines flow. And, the fingers are a part of the Hand. Why do WE ask you to do this? Like your finger, You are a special and wonderful one-of-a-kind perfect human, part of the whole. Now, without one finger, the hand must make adjustments. So, too, the world must make Adjustments without you, and the whole is affected. Are you participating in your World?

Day 147

The second stage of prayer, Thanksgiving: expression of gratitude to US, the universes, for that which you have, have had, and will have.

Day 148

Take time today to just Breathe and Relax!
It is Important for Your Magnificent Being.

Day 149

GOD – Go On Dreaming

Without dreams, no progress.

Without progress, no movement.

Without movement, no future worth dreaming about. If you but dream, you will soar towards that which you call God/Self.

Day 150

If you do not have a set time or place to pray, WE tell you it is alright. Remember, whenever you come WE are waiting with loving arms.

Day 151

Many think depression is a mental disorder. WE tell you, the mental is mostly affected, yet it is a Spiritual matter more than anything else. Yes, oftentimes medication can be used.

However, through spiritual remedies such as prayer, meditation, yoga, Reiki healing, and positive affirmations, many and most cases of Depression can be overcome!

Day 152

Today, reward yourself with laughter. There is nothing more relieving than a good laugh. So watch a funny movie or laugh with your family. Additionally, laughing at oneself is most Therapeutic. Believe it or not.

Day 153

The Studio of Your Mind

Your mind is like a movie studio. Pictures, scenes, and sounds are constantly rushing to and fro within the brain. So every so often, edit your mind. Now what do WE mean?

Well, Meditation is an excellent Editor!

Day 154

It is imperative to note that the concept of Negativity is not natural. Unhappiness is not in your makeup. It has been created by the human mental and reinforced by the emotional. Just like the song, "Don't Worry, Be Happy!"

Day 155

It is not a high vibration to live in fantasy. If you may be prone to fantasy, you must begin to understand that you should be grounded most of the time. Yet know that a little Fantasy is, shall WE say, good for you.

Therefore, Fantasize sometimes, just don't get swept away by it.

Day 156

The third stage of prayer, Petition: expression of your needs and desires. (Note that needs do not necessarily have to be verbally expressed to US, but you can if you like.)

Day 157

Understand that there is a connection to and between your waking life and your dreams.

Day 158

Oh, the sweet, sweet sound of your voice in time of Prayer.

Have you prayed Today?

Day 159

Your neighbors are to be cherished.
Do you know them on an intimate level? If not, get to know them. You never know when and if one of you may need the other.
Visit a neighbor Today.
It will cause a certain raising of vibration.

Day 160

Each day life, as you understand it to be, presents many options and opportunities. Be ready to take the high road. You can do this by understanding your worth. You can be ready for any given situation that occurs.

Day 161

WE desire for you to know that nothing is sacrilegious, and that there are not blunders, just Mis-takes. And with these Mis-takes comes the ability to Re-take or Re-do the scenes, thus causing the Matrix to unfold with different Outcomes and Consequences.

Day 162

Your spirit conceptually understands and is therefore pleased that there is always reciprocation to all of your Prayers, even if the mental portion convinces you to think not. What you have been Praying for and working towards will come to be!

Day 163

The fourth stage of prayer, Intersession: expression of your concern for others and situations in your society at large and your close geo-proximity.

Day 164

Stimulating your brain is essential to growth and the remembrance process. What have you read lately? Reading anything is actually OK. Yet, if you wish to raise your vibrational level and intellect, read something that is thought-provoking.

Day 165

Many have stated that Faith mainly has to do with Theology or Religion, yet this is far from the truth. Sometimes it does have to do with an unseen reality or the belief in what you term as a Supreme Being or US. However, Faith is actually reality based on your own Spiritual Personal Insight, Experience and Authority.

Day 166

Keep putting one foot in front of the other.
Eventually, You will get where You are going.

Day 167

Is there something that you really desire? If so, make a plan to obtain such and go get it. Remember, you are Creator. You are able to bring into being your thoughts. Not many animals on your planet can do so. Therefore, be grateful!

Day 168

Contempt Prior to Investigation

This phrase Underscores the Importance of Checking into things for Yourself before Judgements. It is the Single Most Valuable Undertaking that You Can Do to Improve Your Conditions and Attitudes in Life.

Day 169

If you are Married

~ Have a Date Night!

If you are in a Committed Relationship

~ Have a Date Night!

If you are Single

~ Have a Date Night with Self!

Day 170

Your life is a succession of one decision after another. Take a look at your own decision-making process. If you have not obtained most of the things that you say you desire in life, it may be a good idea to Revamp your Process.

Day 171

Children are fascinating, are they not? Most of you could learn much from your Children. Children don't really care much about the color of one's skin until they are told or informed to be concerned about such.

Day 172

Not too long ago in man's history, one could have slaves. Not too long ago in man's history, women could not vote. Not too long ago in man's history, Jews were led to the slaughter. Yes, not too long ago, many of you were told lies about your others that you bought into.

Have you bought into the Lie that Same-Sex marriages should be condemned?

Day 173

For those such as you that seek Higher Levels of vibration, it is important to know the Following: People Love the Way they Love, not the Way You Think they should. This Revelation in and of itself can assist you in understanding yourself and others better. It will allow you to see others with softer eyes.

Day 174

WE desire for the spectrum of misgivings to cease, thus eliminating future unnecessary pain for many of you. The truth that your Spirit is Forever must be brought to the forefront and into the light. It is time for all to understand that You are Forever!

Day 175

Throughout history, WE have been talking to you. WE spoke through Angels and Messages through Men and Women that many of you simply thought to be insane. WE have giving information for your Soul and information for your Advancement.

Have you been Listening?

Day 176

To not have faith in self is a travesty. Do you believe in your Self? WE believe in you. Take some time and say Positive Affirmations to yourself each day. Tell your friends to do this, inform your children of its worth. It will cause a certain uplifting of the Mass Consciousness.

Day 177

Great structures you have made in the attempts to house US. WE are spirit, WE can't be housed. WE are indeed dwelling within the structures and churches you have built. You can find US there. Fore, WE are outside them and all around them. Yet, Remember, you can find US in the Alley too!

Day 178

Think about when you were a child. Think about the Visions and Dreams that you held for yourself and others. Think about the peaceful world you foresaw.

It's not too Late!

Day 179

Total well-being is important. What have you been eating lately? How is your sleep pattern? When is the last time you visited a Doctor? These are questions you may need to ask yourself on this Day.

Day 180

The fifth stage of prayer, Submission: submitting and accepting the fact that it will come to be, that you can create it.

The stages of prayer are subconscious and related to the universe while praying.

Day 181

Check Your Levels

Just like a car, you need periodic maintenance.

So Today, check the levels of your:

Patience

Tolerance for self and others

Compassion

Day 182

In today's world, many women feel the changing tides. Women everywhere are beginning to understand the need to use their Goddess/God given right and ability of leadership to assist the world in becoming as it should be.

Day 183

What is a Man?

Some will tell you a man should be ready for war and lead his family with a stern hand. WE tell you a man should always allow the Female to lead, Seek Peace, and Guide his household with Love and Affection.

Day 184

Do you take pride in all that your hands do? Well, you should. Each task that you undertake each day should be done with Love in mind. When you do this, you understand that whatever the outcome of your endeavors, all will be well.

Day 185

Your Mother is the vessel from which you appeared on planet Earth. Let her know that you love and appreciate her. If she is still alive, tell her. If she has passed over, exclaim out loud to the universe that you are grateful for her giving you life. WE, All There Is, Was, and Ever Shall Be, will ensure that the memory of her blows in the universal wind.

Day 186

Do you appreciate your Earth?

Well, it would be a good idea to let her/him know! Plant some Flowers or a Tree, pick up some Refuse you see lying around.

Remember, the Earth gives You a bounty of wonders.

Day 187

All of creation has designed itself to take in certain elements, process them, and then give out something different or similar into the cycle of life. Your being is no different. You are designed to take in Air and give out Love.

Day 188

Faith is knowing, it is understanding that that which you believe is. Faith instantaneously sees the Best and Brightest outcome. Faith does not question, faith accepts and clinches to the desired outcome.

Therefore, it Becomes!

Day 189

Fear is unnecessary. Fear brings about inactivity and procrastination. Fear is a tool of lower vibrations to keep You from obtaining great heights. Fear echoes low self-worth and submissive behaviors. Fear can cause You to be overly aggressive, which may bring harm to oneself and others.

Day 190

Millions are waking up, standing up, and remembering that All are One, that they are a part of the Master Plan. Yes, this is an exciting time for the entire human race.

How Woke Are You?

Day 191

What one does, does affect others. You can't escape this fact. Your actions and behaviors may cause countless and lasting effects to your others as well as yourself. With this in mind, the higher vibrational person will think twice before they act or speak.

Day 192

When was the last time you told someone that WE are real? Now, WE don't mean Preaching it to them. What WE mean is have you informed others of their own personal power? Have you told them that all can have their Desires and Dreams Come True?

Day 193

WE tell you that there is enough for all on planet Earth. There always will be.

Day 194

Many have issues with their Fathers. Many fathers did not or are not treating their families very well. Whatever the case may be, Without your Father - You would not be. You would not be able to love, laugh, cry, or do any functions. Therefore, even if You find it hard to tell them, tell US in Prayer you are grateful for them. You will be better off. Trust US!

Day 195

Do you know anyone out of work at this present time? Do you know anyone having a hard time getting by? If you do, encourage them. Check on them. Support them. Love them. If they need help and it is within your means and power, Help them.

Day 196

Music is a gift from US and Yourself to Yourself. Music is for Calming and Stimulation. Music is for Thinking and Pondering. Music can and does, at times, send away insanity.

Day 197

Rain is the cleanser of the Earth. Rain keeps the grass growing. Rain fills your streams and rivers, as well as your oceans. Many times you may forget just how much WE love you. If this occurs, Keep in mind the universe will always ensure that you have Rain.

Is not this wonderful?

Day 198

Teach your Children This!

Teach them that the habit or practice of honoring their bodies gives way to confidence and other positive attributes in adult life. Honoring the body further allows one to be self-assured and leads to less envy and jealousy as an Adult.

Day 199

Just think about how it will be when you are once again able to send high vibrational thoughts to others. (You already do.) WE wish for you to visualize yourself and a friend or loved one finishing each other's sentences.

Day 200

There have been studies on the human body's connection to a full moon, i.e. emergency room visits, animal bites, crime rates, psychiatric, and mental ward check-ins, women's menstrual cycles and sleep deprivation. WE tell you that all of these are affected by the Moon. Mark OUR words; All will come around to a clearer understanding of the undeniable Spiritual Connection to Your Moon.

Day 201

Your mind is a never-ending succession of thoughts. Each day you process literally millions of pieces of data. Each day you analyze and over-analyze many things. Everyday you take apart almost every idea that you have, spin it, turn it over, and spit it back out for some sort of action or non-action.

Day 202

Think you not that each day someone or something, somewhere is watching you? Therefore, be always mindful of all your behaviors and actions.

Day 203

Take a deeper look at your internet, you will see it is a gift from US. There is no other Source that it could have come from. WE desire for your life to be easy. Therefore, WE have always given you the tools to assist you in finding information. WE will always give you routes to obtain another level of education, consciousness, and discernment.

Day 204

WE wish and desire for you to be fully informed, fully informed on and about your choices. Fore, you see, your choices have dictated your past, will dictate your present, and most certainly affect your future.

Day 205

Remember, every once in a while or ever so often, it is a high vibrational choice to do a random act of Compassion and Kindness! Without telling anyone!

If you adhere to this, you will in fact be changing the world one person at a time.

Day 206

How about you Today ~ send Gifts and

Cards to those in Your Life

for no apparent Reason.

You do not have to wait

for a holiday or a Birthday!

Day 207

As you go about your day, today completing your daily Tasks - Know that you are as Wonderful as the Clouds in the Sky. Understand that you are as Majestic as the Rivers and the Mountains. Know and understand that you are a Time Traveler and Shape-Shifter.

Day 208

Many of you ask, "Why should I believe in that which I can't see?" This is a valid question. Why should you? This is the reason that many of you think, "If I can't see God, I will make up an image of what I think God would look like."
And that is OK!
Fore, WE are indeed everything!

Day 209

More Doctors and Medical Professionals are looking into the Incorporation of Homeopathic or Natural Healing to their Practices.

Seek them Out!

Day 210

Magic is only another word for Manifesting that which you Desire without harming Yourself or Your Others.

So, Please all of You - Do Magic!

Day 211

There is No Sin

There Is No Devil

There is No Hell

Yet, there is Reincarnation for the Soul to

Remember - All are Equal

and should be Treated as Such.

If you don't believe anything else,

Believe This. It will Change Your Life.

Day 212

What about days that you are not feeling so good? What should you do? It is best to do the best you can. Sometimes you just have to, shall WE say, suck it up and proceed. On other days, don't do anything. Far too many of you push yourself to the limit or brink of exhaustion. And that Our Dear Ones is Not good, as you understand the term.

Day 213

Take a look at the Crusades and many other wars, which were carried out by men who falsely justified them in OUR name. WE are love, peace and serenity personified. No war is, thus, ever carried out in OUR name except in the minds of men.

Day 214

Know that Great Women and Men all have one thing in Common. When all is Said and Done, they look to the Sky for Answers. How about You?

Day 215

Today in Your Life state -

Nothing is wrong.

I AM alive and present.

I AM able to dictate my actions and behaviors.

I will make the highest choice for myself.

Day 216

You are a continuing Process, a masterpiece in the works. On some days no work is done, on others great strides come into reality on the canvas. WE tell you this for you to understand that it is not a high vibrational choice to get down on yourself during the Process. Just wait until it starts again.

Day 217

WE tell you, it is better to avoid some Others rather than expose yourself to Foolishness that may cause a certain lowering of your personal vibration. Maybe, another day those ones will be at a higher vibration and you will be able to enjoy their company.

Day 218

Global Warming is a concern for many. Your Earth is going through its normal cycle. It just so happens that man was not around the last time this cycle occurred. The good news is, WE have given you and will give to you all the information necessary to sustain life on Earth. Don't Worry!

Day 219

Self-esteem is something that must be worked on. It is a continuing Process. Today, say to Self - There is Nothing I cannot Accomplish. So, it is Uttered, So, it is!

Day 220

All of you desire to be liked by your others; and well you should. However, You don't need anyone's approval, and They don't need Yours. This is a Fact! Accept it and your vibration will change. You will draw towards You those of Like Mind.

Day 221

Are you complicating your Life?

You don't have to.

Day 222

WE spoke before about how sometimes nothing is going on during your Process of Life. Look at it for what it is - Downtime. All of you need a little Downtime. You can only do what you can do, no more, no less.
Know that you will get there. Some parts of the Process takes decades, others a few years.

Day 223

Are you a positive example? Do you have people that gravitate towards your being or do you have people who make attempts to avoid you? The interactions that you have with your others are gauged by them, one of two ways.

Emulation

Avoidance

Which Wave are you Sending out?

Day 224

There are no Sins. However, there are Seven Lower Vibrational Decisions one can make.

7. Pride - You should look this up in The Sapiential Discourses, Book III, pg. 111.

Day 225

It is imperative to know that sexuality is a part of your reality. Help children to understand this fact. Assist them in understanding the ways your society views sexuality so they may make high vibrational choices for themselves. Teach them the truth.

Day 226

Fore, remember all is holy, even those things or persons which include but are not limited to inanimate beings. (There is no such thing as an abomination to God, US.) If anyone tells you differently they are lying to you.

Day 227

The real trick to meditation is to listen to your inner voice or the voice of the universe, US. The mental portion of one's being has to be slowed down for the spiritual to take the lead and connect with the universe, which will provide the answers sought.

Day 228

If you have a Soul Mate in this current life of yours, do the following: Join with them in love and compassion. Stick with them through thick and thin. Come what may, do not give up on them or your sacred self.

Tolerate their mistakes and misgivings. Care for them as you would yourself.

Day 229

Are you celebrating your life?

Each of you should celebrate your life, the things that you have accomplished and the many joys that you have.

Day 230

If you are in a Romantic Relationship, ensure that you Touch your significant other Often in a Sensual manner, for no apparent reason. It will keep the Flame of Passion burning, and if the Fire has gotten small, it will bring about a Blaze.

Day 231

Bullying - No one likes to be put down. People need to be respected. With this being said - What are you teaching your children? Do you talk to them about Loving others? Do you put down others in front of them? Do you make derogatory remarks about people you see on TV or in Movies? These are good questions to ask yourself as you navigate your offspring on the Road of Life.

Day 232

If You are prone to Stress, it can be dealt with in many ways. One can work it off with exercise and sports. Self-help groups are a common and popular tool used for relieving stress. Talking to a friend or relative helps in many cases. Of course, WE would prefer that You use prayer, yoga, laughter, journaling, sleep, and meditation.

Day 233

Jesus unbeknownst to many said -

All of you are messiahs, messiahs for anyone

at any given Time!

Day 234

Today, think about a world of peace, visualize it, call it into being. YOU have the Power!

Day 235

Twin Flames are for Reflection, Guidance, Important Spiritual Communications, and Dream State Reality Checks.

But, <u>Not for Long Term</u> Sexual Relationships.

Day 236

Is your house clean, your car, your yard? Do you take pride in the them? Do you enjoy the work you do? How are your intimate relationships? Do you give of yourself to others? The answers to these questions are good indicators of where your head is at.

Day 237

Social injustice also applies to your treatment of animals, fore, they are your charges as set by the universe. They too depend on you as you depend on them. They do not neglect you, do they? No! They give you food, laughter, beauty to view, and excitement. Therefore, you should treat them as such, a part of you.

Day 238

When you pray, are your prayers for others? People all over your world need your prayers. Prayer is one of the most Powerful Tools for Change. Prayer does make a Difference.
Believe US.

Day 239

Now Think About the following:

Each of You have had a minimum of

777,777 Lifetimes.

Now the questions are -

When were they?

Where were they?

Day 240

Everything that occurs in this life of yours is for your Remembering Process. Everything is about Your Connection to Others and US. Yes, there is Reason and Purpose for all Things. All Events and Encounters are to Help You in Your Process.

Day 241

Do you remember Y2K? All the fuss and Commotion? People everywhere were in lines buying water, batteries and the like. Mass hysteria was at hand. So too, people will be worried over many things. As a Seeker of Truth, please, do not feed into hysteria in the Days to come.

Day 242

What about the people who are prisoners in their own minds, or those being held captive by abusive husbands or parents? How about those that don't have Freedom in your world. WE think you should send out a Loud Verbal request to the Angels to assist all that are not Free.

Day 243

Perseverance is needed to succeed in your endeavors. In baking a cake, building a tree house or crocheting a scarf; a certain drive must be present. Many have uncompleted projects and dreams are set aside and forgotten. If you begin a task, it is ok to take a break or stop a project and never go back. Yet, the question is for each of you - How important is it to You?

Day 244

Everything is sound and vibration. Many at this time do not wish to see, accept, and acknowledge the connection of sounds to the human body and the universe in general. Do you feel the connection?

Day 245

Intent is everything. What are your intentions? This is a question that you should ask yourself at the start of almost anything you do. For goals to be met or decisions to be made, it is a good idea to ask Yourself, "Why am I doing this? What do I expect?"

Day 246

Mermaids and Dolphins were a part of Atlantis. And they are now helpers to humans in many ways. Perhaps you should look into Dolphins and their connection to humans.

Also, investigate the Mermaid.

You may be surprised what you find.

Day 247

All on planet Earth have Freedom of Choice. Now, the general map of Your Life has been set. However, the reactions and behaviors that you may exhibit cannot be Foretold and this can or may affect where you go on Your Life's Map. Some Actions can take you far away from the road that you should be on.

Day 248

Sometimes people treat their pets better than they treat their family members. Do you know anyone that does this?

Day 249

Gardening is something that must be done with love. Each plant needs fertilizer, water, proper sunlight, and so forth and so on. Relationships are the same. They require love, conversation, listening, and nurturing.

Do you tend to your Relationships properly?

Day 250

Events in your news can be disheartening. Unfortunately, there is always some lower vibrational activity that takes place. However, if you watch or read long enough, you will see a positive story that will cause joy in your Spirit. Fore, Remember, The Good Always outnumbers what you would consider the Bad!

Day 251

FYI - Those that Channel US at the highest apex, those that Channel other portions of US in some form, and those that are Healers are affected more than others by Schumann Waves. The level of these waves ranges from 7.9 Hz to 25.0 Hz. Additionally, 25.0 Hz is the fourth Harmonic that affects the Crown Charka and the Third Eye.

Day 252

Love is understanding that you are a Creator, able to reach the Stars if you but wish. Love is Family and Laughter. Love is Pain and Pleasure, Sorrow and Smiles.

Day 253

You can stop guessing now. Life starts at the moment of fusion (or fertilization) of an ovum (egg) with a sperm. It is from this time on that Freedom of Choice begins in everything you do. WE mean everything.

Day 254

In any sport, the goal is to score points. Your life is not a game. You don't have to score points as many of you have been informed. There is no need to punch it through the goal or destroy your opponent.

All you have to do is be, yes, be the best you can during any given situation.

Day 255

Do Something Special

for the One You

Love Today.

That One Could be YOU!

Day 256

Democritus formulated an atomic theory of the cosmos; Plato - the first institution of higher learning. Aristotle - a founding figure of western philosophy. Pythagoras made strides in mathematics and philosophy, he is noted for the Pythagorean Theorem. WE tell you faith caused all these things to be. And it is Faith that will take you where you are going.

Day 257

Do you feel your Angels?

Yes, there are Angels. They guide you gently, they push you softly towards higher vibrational choices. Angels can't be seen, yet, they are all around you!

Day 258

The revelations of internal and external questions to one's self can be as a nova, bursting out into the universe. This is how one should feel after opening up to new possibilities and receiving the epiphanies that can and will occur during a good meditation.

Day 259

Many suffer from Substance Abuse. All of you have been touched in one way or another by this. What can you do to help or assist someone who is dealing with such? Nothing, except - inform them that they have other choices and, do not enable their negative self to continue on a path to personal destruction.

Day 260

Some may wish or desire to debate today's words. Don't believe for one moment that the hunted animal does not know its day of capture or death. You would be greatly mistaken.

Freedom of Choice is for Animals too!

Day 261

Go outside, pick up a handful of dirt. Take a look at it, feel it, let it run through your fingers. Notice the consistency. Place it back down on Mother/Father Earth. Or just throw it down or let it blow in the wind, it matters not. What does matter is that you Understand, that You are It and It is You!

Day 262

Did you realize that more people are attending comedy shows? This is an unspoken desire of Ours. All of You should understand the need for more laughter in your life and in your world.

Have you had a good laugh Today?

Day 263

Do Not Live in Fear! There are people who fear touching objects, they fear the contraction of some disease. Know that WE have given you the tools to combat germs that do not or should not be within and on your bodies. You should investigate to find out what they are.

Remember, knowledge is Power!

Day 264

There are no Sins. However, there are Seven Lower Vibrational Decisions one can make.

5. Wrath - You should look this up in The Sapiential Discourses, Book III, pg. 111.

Day 265

Some think that they have nothing to celebrate. However, WE tell each of you that there are many portions of your existence that you can be joyous about. Do you have a job, relationships, a car, a house or apartment? Do you have friends, pets, any form of entertainment? Think about it.

Day 266

Many have and will tell you that

OUR Reason and Purpose is to be

Adored and Worshipped.

WE need not worship.

However, WE would like

for you to love all others!

Day 267

Faith has been said to be the mental assurance of things not seen. This is true, yet it is also the assurance of things Seen that may be hoped for, dreamed of, and envisioned within Your Conscious and Subconscious Self.

Day 268

If you don't take care of yourself,

what do you think will happen?

You will break down.

If you don't take care of the Earth,

What do You think will Happen?

Day 269

Some of you need a vacation, you need to step outside your everyday life, and see the world. It is important to see how many of your others live in order to understand them better.

When was the last time you took a vacation?

Day 270

If you suffer from low self-esteem and low self-worth, Do the following: Get a sheet of paper. Write down all of your Personal Assets, and <u>WE</u> don't mean <u>monetary.</u> Go over them and see your worth as a human being. Fore, You are Wonderful!

Day 271

New and exciting avenues will open up for You. Understand that life is unfolding for you right in front of your eyes. Be alert for new opportunities to grow Spiritually, they are always present. Work on being open-minded to new ways of thinking and behaving as long as it jeopardizes not your safety or security!

Day 272

When is the last time you really listened to the words of songs on the radio? Do a project and see what people are singing today. Remember the songs that you grew up on. If you do so, you will most certainly Remember that Nothing is New Under the Sun.

Day 273

You are an analytical being. WE, the universe, made you as such. WE formed you to be able to problem-solve and handle any given number of Scenarios at any given time.

See! You are absolutely Superb.

And WE would have it no other way.

Day 274

If one is able to obtain the state of being free of worry, that one's life, as you understand the term, will be better. Fore, why worry about anything, especially death? It comes to all living things, it is a part of the Process!

Day 275

Do you know how many stars there are? WE tell you, the number is impossible for you to calculate. WE bring this up to you this day to assist you in understanding that, just as the number of stars in the midnight sky is mind-boggling, so too are the possibilities for Your Life!

Day 276

7 - Seven is a very important number. The moon has seven phases. Your body has seven orifices and seven major chakras. The brain has seven major functions. The body has seven major organs. It would be a good idea for you to look these things up for yourself to understand the importance of the number 7.

Day 277

Jesus unbeknownst to many said -

I Am the Son of God.

Yet still,

All of You,

are the Sons and Daughters of God.

Day 278

Karma - Some of you do not really understand what karma is. Karma is the consequence of actions connected to one of you not accepting Everything and Everyone just as it is, Equal to all others. The failure to accomplish this brings about another lifetime.

Day 279

Jesus unbeknownst to many said -

Each day is Holy - Not Just the Sabbath.

Each day a Life can be Saved

Or Someone's Vibration can be Raised.

Day 280

Do you know how important Breakfast is? It is perhaps the most important meal of the day. Children especially need Breakfast. On you own, it would be a good idea to research the nutritional value of this meal and adjust accordingly. Remember, like a car, your body needs Fuel!

Day 281

Faith is confident understanding or trust in a person, concept, or idea without having what you would call Proof.

Day 282

Memories Last - Reach out Today or soon to some of your childhood friends and Reminisce. Those days, in fact, helped to shape you into who and what you are today. It is a high vibrational choice to keep one foot slightly in the past to remember and ensure that you do not forget From Whence You Came.

Day 283

Let your love flow because you desire and wish for them to spend silent moments with US alone, apart from you.

Day 284

Many isolate themselves from the rest of the world. Isolation is good for one in small doses. It is therapeutic, every once in awhile, to recollect your thoughts and ponder your next moves in life. However, prolonged isolation is not a high vibrational choice.

Day 285

Understand that all it takes,

oftentimes, is to look the one or ones

that you need to express some feeling or

emotion to in the eyes and say

~ This is important to Me!

You may be surprised at the outcome.

Day 286

There are no Sins. However, there are Seven Lower Vibrational Decisions one can make.

2. Gluttony - You should look this up in *The Sapiential Discourses*, Book III, pg. 111.

Day 287

Sometimes you may be attacked verbally and provoked to engage in some lower vibrational debate or activity. These attacks may come from someone you love. During these times, seek within yourself not to go there with them. Yet, if you do, Don't Beat Yourself Up, and try not to repeat the Behavior Again.

Day 288

A Vision Board is a wonderful tool to assist you in seeing and bringing about your dreams and desires. Vision Boards are not hard to make. A law of the universe is that if you can see it, you can bring it to fruition.

Why not make a Vision Board for Yourself?

Day 289

How are you with money? Do you save? Have you saved any money lately? Now, of course, you can't take it with you. It may be a good idea to have a little for emergencies. If you don't, do not worry about it. Just look for and plan for the day that you will have something set aside, "Just In Case."

Day 290

Pain is good, as you understand the term. Pain lets one know that healing is coming. If the burn is not painful the healing will not come. If the pain of losing a relationship did not come, one would not know when to move on, when to let go. Yes, it is the non-acceptance of pain that brings about the suffering.

Day 291

Come to the remembrance and understanding that the universe has not given you any set conditions for prayer, any time limitations or restrictions. There are no parameters or guidelines, no certain amount of words that must be spoken in any given order.

Day 292

Putting others first, in many cases, actually ensures that you receive that which you need. Remember, all are one. If you are truly concerned for others and wish them to be happy, you will understand that caring for yourself will allow you to help others.

Day 293

Did you know that movement is vital to your physical being? If you stay in one spot and never move, your muscles will begin to atrophy. The mind, emotions, and spiritual parts of you too, should likewise always be moving, changing, improving, growing. Solving problems, feeling your emotions and spiritual connections to your others will keep your total being from atrophy.

Day 294

You will find many theories why people yawn. Studies into the rhymes and reasons for yawning have not been conclusive as of yet by man.

Guess what? That's the way WE planned it.

Yet, WE will inform you that it is a needed function. Now, before the year 3547 the information will be given. Why 3547? Well, that is when mankind will need to understand.

Day 295

When you are feeling stressed-out or think you are unable to continue, Breathe!

Deep breaths increase the flow of oxygen in your being and cause a certain surge in energy. So if you find yourself vey anxious about something, Remember to Breathe!

Day 296

Children are a joy by design of the universe and you. Children have been given to you as charges. Children are for you to pass on all that you have remembered.

Are you passing along your high vibrational Remembrances or something else?

Day 297

When you think you can't go on, keep going. When you feel you are at the end of your rope, WE provide more rope. When you think all is lost, you shall be found. If you think you are alone, think again. If you look to the sky, all your answers will fall down to you like Manna from what you have been told are the heavens.

Day 298

Contemplate this: Everything that happens on your Earth is by choice. It is by the choice of one of you or all of you. This may be unsettling to many of you, yet, it is true. Therefore, Remember, your choices affect you and all your others. There is a thread that runs through the Matrix of the Universes that connects all thoughts and actions.

Day 299

Your Aunts and Uncles, if you have them, are in your direct Bloodline. They are your mother's and your father's extensions in the flesh. Today, make an effort to call your Aunts and Uncles.

WE are so glad you are taking out the time for self.

WE Love You

Day 300

Tears are a gift from US and from You to your Wonderful Self. Tears are meant to Flow in times of pain and times of great joy. Tears are meant to flow quite often.

It is by design.

Day 301

"You are either going into a Storm or Coming out of one!" WE say, your life is unpredictable, you never know what might happen. If you are fit Spiritually, it does not matter. If a storm or troubling times occur, you will be equipped. If you are in touch with Self and US, storm or not, you will stay afloat.

Day 302

Take some time Today to think about what you wish or desire for the rest of this Year!

Now, make it happen!

Day 303

There are no Sins. However, there are Seven Lower Vibrational Decisions one can make.

3. Greed - You should look this up in The Sapiential Discourses, Book III, pg. 111.

Day 304

Are you one to enjoy that which your hands have brought about, or are you one to only store and accumulate, never taking the opportunity to appreciate what you have been blessed with?

Day 305

Some Trees are like many of you. They grow, on their own without supervision or tending to. However, Trees give back to the whole, They are a part of the process of Photosynthesis giving important carbons and oxygen back into the atmosphere. Even if you grew up on your own, or have had to fend for yourself for many years, what are you giving back to the whole?

Day 306

People Pleasing? If so, you may wish to ponder the fact that People will either like you or they won't. Remember, there is Freedom of Choice.

Now this may seem like a harsh fact. If you think about it, a conclusion that you don't like everyone, will come. Notice WE said like. You must Love all. Love, is the key to Understanding. Love is a Paradox and Enigma!

Day 307

If you have children in the teenage years, it is a good idea to at least have some idea of what they are involved in. Far too often in today's society, many parents have no idea what their children are really into. Spend time talking to your teenage children. It is most important!

Day 308

Resentments are a silent Killer. Resentments drag the spirit downwards, and cause all sorts of discomforts and diseases. Resentments are like an untreated tumor. Resentments fester and grow in darkness. Do you have any resentments? If so, get rid of them.

Day 309

It is the neglecting of your spirit or its voice

that many of you do not adhere to.

This is very detrimental to your entire being.

Ask yourself - Do I pay attention

to the voice within?

Day 310

Prayer does cause Mountains of Lies to be Moved and Bridges of Hate to Crumble. Prayer does Put Food in the Mouths of Many. Prayer has the Power of US, yes, God within it. Pray today for your World and Everyone Upon the Face of Her/Him!

Day 311

Honesty

Practicing honesty is most rewarding.

Do you practice honesty with self and others?

Do you sometimes find yourself telling yourself half-truths and little lies?

It is a part of the human condition to do so. Today and Everyday tell yourself the truth.

Day 312

If everyone agreed with you all of the time, you would go insane. Each of you needs sounding boards that do not always reflect back the exact same ideas and thoughts that you sent out. Today be grateful that all in the universe does not agree with you all the time!

Day 313

If you always do the same Practices, the same Patterns, you will always get the same results. Sometimes the Practices are Flawed and the results are not what you really need. This means, they should not be repeated. Today switch your Practices and Patterns you might be Pleased with the Outcomes.

Day 314

Today would be a good day to get out and view nature. Get out of your house or apartment and appreciate the Beauty all around You!

Day 315

The mental only sees what it thinks is in front of it. Thus, when it is presented with pain or painful situations it first, goes into flee mode. If the spiritual portion is strong, it will convince the mental portion not to flee, to take a rational look at what is really occurring. This allows You to make choices that will at best attack the dis-ease and the symptoms.

Day 316

Did you know that -

Meditation can and does allow one to move, so to speak, in and out of self, transcending time and space.

Day 317

Do you question yourself? Do you second guess your answers and thoughts almost all of the time? If you are, stop doing so. That is, unless the thought or answer will harm you or others. Most original thoughts are what you really wish to say to self or others. If you are on a high vibration, if you pray, meditate, and Breathe, you need not fear your original thoughts.

Day 318

All of you have the ability to use your ESP. Each of you is able to see into the future if you really desire to. You were meant to connect to your others and the entire universe on an unspoken level.

Day 319

There are many words that express the feelings WE experience in totality when you come to US in prayer. Some are: blissful, delighted, pleasure, enjoyment, refreshment, fortunate, magical, nascent, trustful, jazzy, honored, reassured, awarded, convivial, and relevant. Come to US Today!

Day 320

Have you ever wondered why sometimes if you have been raising your vibrational level, you feel uncomfortable in your own skin? WE tell you, it is what you would consider natural. Remember, the Spirit always seeks release, for it is in true reality a most unnatural state for your Spirit to be within a Body.

Day 321

Today WE ask you to reflect on just how far

you have come since being in the 6th grade.

If you really think about it,

You have come a very long way!

Day 322

The Sublime Law of Forever

You are Forever, the Trees are Forever, the Flowers are Forever, the Mountains are Forever, the Rivers are Forever, the Stars Are Forever. All is Forever. And Everything, Everywhere is Attempting to remain Current in some Form or another in Hopes of Reunification with US in Totality.

Day 323

WE inform You that there are many Falsehoods and Questionable statements in the Bible. However, "Honor your Father and your Mother," is not one of them. In doing so you are in fact honoring Yourself.

Day 324

Are You Allowing those close to You

to experience - Intimacy?

Into Me You See

Day 325

Please, if you would think about the following:

An emotional void can occur if you become stuck in the false idea or belief of being abandoned. Simply, because you are never alone, and can never really be left alone. So, the highest vibrational choice is to accept that the perceived abandonment is not true.

Day 326

There are no Sins. However, there are Seven Lower Vibrational Decisions one can make.

6. Envy - You should look this up in The Sapiential Discourses, Book III, pg. 111.

Day 327

If active Prayer is avoided,

the spirit will not flourish.

How is your Prayer Life?

Day 328

If you read with the whole-word method, what you read enters the Right Hemisphere of your brain. It does not understand language or words. Then the word read goes to the Left Hemisphere of the brain, which does understand words and language. There it is translated and transferred back to the right side for storage, compartmentalization, Memory, and understanding.

Day 329

If you read with the phonetic method, what you read enters the Left Hemisphere of your brain, which understands the word, its sound or language. Then it is transferred to the Right Hemisphere of the brain where it is stored for future use and understanding. This method is the smoothest and most fluent way of reading.

Day 330

The word Love has throughout time, had a variety of meanings, yet really only one. Its meaning is universal. Intuitively, you already know what Love is not. Therefore, you really know what it is - Everything.

Day 331

There are no Sins. However, there are Seven Lower Vibrational Decisions one can make.

4. Laziness - You should look this up in The Sapiential Discourses, Book III, pg. 111.

Day 332

So the question is,

When is the last time you cried?

OUR dear ones, Remember, you were not meant to hold it all in. Therefore, Release and be Balanced within Self!

Day 333

Remember, if you have school children, check their homework from time to time. It is important to keep in the know. Are you progressively ensuring that your child completes his or her homework if they have such?

If you have no school age children or no children - Watch a Movie Tonight!

Day 334

Who is your idol? Do you have one?

Many people put others up on pedestals.

After those that they have placed in high regards let them down, many become jaded.

WE tell you - If you don't put them on the pedestal, They can't Fall Off!

Day 335

Children learn by example and repetition. They always have and always will, so why not make it fun? Group interaction is one of the best ways to present concrete, sound, loving ideas, and concepts.

Day 336

Did you know that Mandalas, sacred geometric drawings or images are infused with Sound and Vibrations? The word means Circle in Sanskrit. When Drawn, Colored, or Viewed, they Send Out High Vibrations that affects the Mental portion of your being. This causes the Spiritual portion to be Happy.

Day 337

FYI - Gongs originated in early African civilizations. Gongs were designed to calm the mind. Their tones have a connection to dopamine and the electrical impulses that are sent to the entire body.

Day 338

Want to hear something funny?

Many believe that some of you are not worthy of receiving communication from US or able to discern the information if it does come.

Many think only a few can give the information to the Masses. Further, many think that if WE send messages, it must be given to someone who is considered to be a Saint.

Day 339

When is the last time you did a complete
and thorough cleaning of the inside
of your House or Apartment?
How about Today or Tomorrow Morning?

Day 340

This day think about this:

To Thy Own Self Be True.

Are you true to Self?

Day 341

You have come a long way Spiritually since you started this book. You have grown by Leaps and Bounds. You have thought about some things that you normally would not think about.

Day 342

Recurring Dreams - These dreams are mainly for you to remember something very important. So if you experience them and remember, take a deeper look at the dream and find out what you are trying to tell yourself. WE give you a clue, it will always be something that is in Your Highest Good.

Day 343

Techniques vary for meditation because of free will. And of course, WE would have it no other way. You can meditate while running, swimming, eating, dancing, or walking.

Remember to Meditate Every Day!

Day 344

With faith, one will begin to change their mindset. One will begin to research and read more. One will begin to watch and listen to more positive input from media tools. Faith will bring about action of the spirit transformed through the physical.

Day 345

There are many more new marvels that all of you will see and be a part of, many things that you do not understand now will come to fruition and light. New information is coming to you each and every day. New discoveries are happening as you read these very words. You will be amazed at what is coming.

Day 346

Notice how Geese protect each other. If there are a pair of Geese, and the female is nesting, the male will stand guard with vigilance. He will watch, and if any intruders come close he will make a ruckus for all to hear. Fathers, are you protecting, watching over your families? When danger is at hand, do you make some noise for all to hear?

Day 347

Remember, there is nothing you can't have, nothing you can't do! There is nothing you can't accomplish if you but wish and desire to.

You are CREATOR!

Day 348

Natural human bonding is driven by chemicals, the thoughts of pleasing or some consideration for the other's feelings are there, i.e. cooking for them, buying a gift, opening the door, etc., and so forth and so on. Yes, it is primal in nature (mating). The is a Mate or Mates for Everyone!

Day 349

Love is the sun that rises in the east and sets in the west. Love is the wind in your hair. Love is the first time you saw him or her. Love is the look in your mother's eyes. Love is a warm cup of coffee and a big bowl of ice cream. Love is the look in the puppy's eyes. Love is all things.

Day 350

Why not surprise your loved one and suggest a nice quiet dinner. Gaze into each others eyes and remember when you first fell in Love.

Day 351

When or if you leave your house Today, Smile at everyone you may come across and see what happens. You never know how your smile will affect another. And you will most certainly cause the spirit within them and yourself to soar towards the Heavens.

Day 352

Do you have friend or relative that may be having a hard time dealing with someone or some situation? Are they experiencing difficult times in their life? It might be a good idea to give them a call Today and encourage them.

Day 353

One day you will cease worrying about if the bills are paid. You will cease caring about whether you have enough money in the bank. All concerns about war and depletion of the Earth's atmosphere will cease in your mind.

That day will be when you decide it to be. It could be Today or Tomorrow!

Qué será, será - Whatever will be, will be!

Day 354

In reality there is no atheist or agnostic, the very concepts of the words prevent such. One can state they do not believe in anything they wish. It is the glory of freedom of choice, yet it will never prevent a thing from being. Therefore, if any of you wish to lay claim to US not being, OUR very being allows one to make the claim and suffer no penalty.

Day 355

Ponder on These Words this Day! So as the snow falls with many flakes, so too has your Journey been back to US. Some have been as a sprinkle of snow and then you return to US. Some have been as a light cover, here today and back to US tomorrow. And many have been as a full-blown storm, inches upon inches and feet upon feet of snow.

Day 356

Are there people you get sick and tired of listening to? Do you literally cringe when they speak? Well, this means you should work on your tolerance. Fore, you say things that you know not what you speak, and do many things that upset someone without you knowing. The next time you are intolerant Think - Is someone intolerant of me?

Day 357

How is your sleeping?

Are you getting enough rest?

Are you overworking?

Are you eating enough?

Are you eating too little?

Are you taking care of yourself?

Day 358

What Season are you in?

Each of you have seasons also. Some seasons are productive, others not so much. The trick, if you like, is the ability to notice the changes in season and prepare to be ready for come what may. Are you ready?

Day 359

Find out for yourself just how much sleep you really need to be at your best. Remember, only you can determine this. No one else knows your body like you do. Fore, it is, after all, your body.

Day 360

As your children grow older your relationships with them should go through a natural progression. Their dependence on you should shift and a deep respect for you will develop. If you have done a good job, you and your children will have a lasting enduring bond. They will let you in on their adult life and you will feel fulfilled as a parent.

Day 361

Self-esteem has a lot to do with guilt. If one's self-esteem is low, that person may take on what is actually the responsibility of another. The person with low self-worth may think, "That is my fault too." It is important to Remember that each of you must take responsibility for your actions and yours alone.

Day 362

Some think that only those with degrees from University are smart. Yet WE tell you, it is not book knowledge that makes up the intellectual complexion of an individual, but the Spiritual Readiness to accept those things that are true. Fore, one can have false knowledge and be as a fool.

Day 363

Remember, if things are not looking good, just around the corner is an answer. Are you one to turn around before turning the corner that will lead you to your intended destination?

Day 364

A Project for You

The more you know the more you grow.

Look into just how many colors there really are.

You will be absolutely Amazed.

Day 365

You Can't stay away from US, no matter how hard you try. What you resist persists, especially US. WE hear your prayers. WE are with you in meditations. In your times of worry, WE are there. In your triumphs, WE are there. When you are sad, there WE are. In times of sickness and in health, there WE are by your side. At your lowest points, next to you, are WE!

One year, 365 Days with Source, words of Comfort and Wisdom have you endured. Some of the words, concepts and ideas in this book were meant to push you to Think. Many of the words were designed to make you uncomfortable, so you can look at yourself and the world around you.

Many of the words were joyous and uplifting. Some of the words may not apply to you now. Some of the words will apply later. Whatever, the case may be. You have, if you picked up this book daily, or every other day, or once a week, or once a month, been in direct contact, through words with the Source of All Things, God, Yourself! And you have done well. You should be proud of yourself. Source Loves You so very, very, much and we do too!

Elliott and Diane Jackson

You Are as a Star in the Midnight Sky.
Keep Shining

We Love You!

Made in the USA
Lexington, KY
06 May 2018